The Gresley Artists
James, Frank, Cuthbert and Harold

by Audrey Longdon

Published by Chellaston History Group

Published in 2010 by Chellaston History Group.

Printed & bound by
Eight Days a Week Print Solutions Ltd.
3 Church View, Canal Side, Ilkeston Rd,
Sandiacre, Nottingham, NG10 5EA

ISBN 978-0-9533410-2-3

Dedicated to the memory of
Dennis Godfrey Longdon

CONTENTS

Foreword

The talented Gresley painters were possessed of a skill and occupation much envied by many: whether driven by financial needs or the urge of a satisfying hobby is beside the point. What is undeniable is that they have left posterity a wonderful collection of paintings to be enjoyed by subsequent generations. The family was unusual in that it produced so many gifted individuals. Theirs was a time-consuming interest spent in the solitude of the countryside recording scenes and activities, many of which have long since disappeared under the weight of progress and development in the 20th and 21st centuries.

A good painting should draw the attention of the viewers to the scenes depicted. They will admire the colours, the detail and techniques used by the artist. It will capture their interest and anyone viewing a Gresley painting will appreciate and be impressed by all those qualities brought out in their brushwork and composition.

They captured in their paintings the agricultural life that had existed for hundreds of years, where work was animal-driven before the advent of modern farming machinery. When corn was "stooked" at harvest time and loaded, horse drawn wagons moved up and down quiet country lanes, whilst farms were still surrounded by neat haystacks and poultry of all kinds freely roamed. Men wearing smocks and gaiters drove farm animals along quiet un-congested roads to market, whilst wives and children helped gather the harvest in.

The Gresleys have recorded such scenes in vivid watercolours, a life that has almost disappeared: country cottages with thatched roofs, and muddy streets not yet covered in tarmac. It was a time when villages were divided from each other by green rolling fields before being mopped up by the expanding towns, built on and destroyed, to become part of an urban sprawl.

Cuthbert, the skilful flower painter, often painted compositions of the local flora but is probably better known for his painting on the fine china of the Royal Crown Derby factory. It is now treasured and much sought after by collectors of fine porcelain.

The Gresleys must have derived much pleasure from their work. They painted the pictures and sold them for very modest amounts even by the standards of their day. It was left to future generations to benefit financially from the sale of their efforts. They would be very proud and flattered to hear the comments of the present owners of their work.

Arthur Shardlow
Chairman
Chellaston History Group

Acknowledgements

Grateful thanks are due to the following:

The late Miss Betty Forman for her background information and encouragement. Stuart and Alan Gresley for photographs and information sent from Australia. Mark Young, Manager, Derby Local Studies Library. Derbyshire County Record Office, Matlock. Sarah Allard, former Keeper of Fine Art, Derby Museums and Art Gallery. Nottingham City Museums and Galleries for permission to photograph and reproduce paintings. Jacqueline Smith, Curator, Royal Crown Derby Museum. Derby Evening Telegraph for permission to reproduce photographs. The many friends who have allowed me to include the paintings from their private collections. Ian Neish and Susan Smith for reading the book in proof and making valuable suggestions. Arthur Shardlow for his generous help, photography, sound advice and for kindly writing the foreword for this book. Tom Greenhouse for his advice and transportation. Huw Meredith for professional photography of pictures. John Twitchett and Betty Wherry for permission to reproduce the image of Cuthbert from their book "Royal Crown Derby". Christopher Forman for permission to use his painting. Alan Foster for photography. Marion Johnson for advice. Mark Tittley for permission to print the image of his house. Derbyshire Community Foundation – Grassroots Grants for their generous contribution to help towards the publication and printing costs. Eight Days a Week Print Solutions for the printing of this book. Lastly, but by no means least, my daughter Cathryn for all the support and help she has given me in the research of this book.

DISCLAIMER

This book has been produced to illustrate the range and artistic talents of the artists involved. It was not possible to photograph all examples of their work under ideal conditions and it is acknowledged that some images do not do full justice to the originals.

THE GRESLEYS

A FAMILY OF ARTISTS

INTRODUCTION

Lovers of art in Derbyshire will surely be familiar with the charming watercolour paintings created by members of the talented Gresley family. Their work consisted of landscapes in watercolour or oil, portraits and exquisitely fine work painted on Royal Crown Derby china.

If one could choose the ideal location to read or talk about the Gresley family, it would surely be at Swarkestone beside the gracefully flowing river Trent, with the fine old bridge in view, the water gleaming and gurgling in the sunlight and a froth of fleecy white clouds floating in a blue summer sky. We would need to see cattle watering in the shallows, a dog on the river bank, perhaps an angler casting his line and in the background an ancient church tower among trees. Amid surroundings such as this, we may recapture some of the tranquil atmosphere of the Gresley landscape paintings.

My own particular interest in the Gresleys and their work stems from the fact that I grew up in the Chellaston area, knew the family and learned to recognise and appreciate the pictures from quite an early age.

The ancient village of Chellaston, where the family lived from about 1893 to 1967, is situated some five miles south of Derby. There have been vast alterations made since the Gresleys first came to reside there. Indeed, until the end of the Second World War, Chellaston remained a truly rural village. Since that time, many new housing estates have been built and sadly, the village has lost a lot of its old world identity and character. Now, we see Chellaston as a mere suburb of Derby but in Victorian times it was a small farming community with one village thoroughfare called "Town Street" and an alabaster and plaster industry which gave employment to many of the villagers. At that time, the railway served Chellaston and this was the only method of public transport to and from Derby for the residents of the village. The more affluent families may have been fortunate enough to own a pony and trap. Otherwise, which is more than likely, they walked! The old parish church of St. Peter, was, in Victorian times, the hub of the village, together with the Methodist and Baptist Chapels, the board school and the three pubs, which were "The Rose and Crown", "The New Inn" and "The Red Lion".

Probably the main reason for the Gresleys moving to Chellaston , would have been its close proximity to the rural, undulating beauty of the Trent Valley and the surrounding picturesque villages of Swarkestone, Barrow-on-Trent, Ingleby, Twyford and Kings Mills: places which the Gresley artists loved to portray in their work, together with the softly running river Trent.

In spite of the changes which have come to Chellaston with the march of time, the family home "Crow Tree House", in School Lane, still remains and, although much altered in character, it still stands to remind us of the artistically talented individuals who once lived there. A plaque, bearing the names of the artists, and provided by the Chellaston History Group, has been placed on the house.

In recent times, there have been numerous exhibitions devoted to the works of England's major artists of the nineteenth and early twentieth centuries. Besides these large scale, wonderful exhibitions of the well known painters, there have been presentations all around the country showing the works of lesser known artists of the period, whose work has given much enjoyment and who, in their different ways, have added to the general picture of landscape painting during that period. The Gresleys of Chellaston fall into this category of minor artists, and although they come nowhere near the hierarchy of British painters, there can be few families that have produced a similar succession of four gifted artists. Their paintings give to our present generation a glimpse of the Victorian and early 20th Century scene before it was scarred by the march of time.

The 19th century was the golden age of English art, producing the well known artists Turner, Constable, Millais, Landseer, Rossetti, Leighton and Holman Hunt. All these artists lived during the reign of Queen Victoria. England's imperial, political, naval and mercantile power reached its peak at this time and likewise produced a brilliance in the artistic world. British art of this period was recognised, not only by the English critics, but also by foreign writers and today such paintings have become an integral part of the traditional Victorian scene.

In an age when we are surrounded by the noise of modern living, to sit back and meditate upon a gentle Gresley landscape is like being transported back through time to an age of peaceful serenity. I have endeavoured in the following pages to describe something of the lives and work of this gifted family and hope that their charming pictures and decorative painting on china will be appreciated by new generations and for many more years to come.

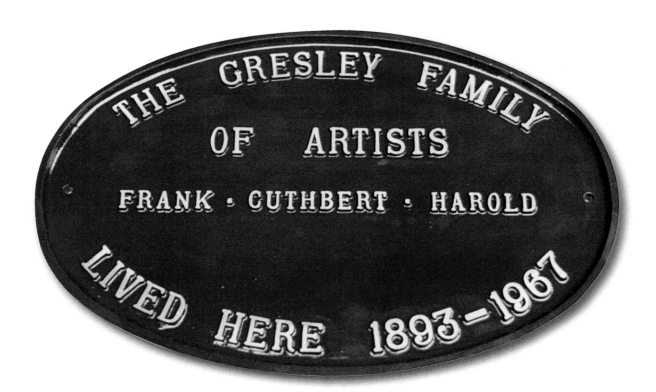

Plaque placed on Crow Tree House in School Lane, Chellaston by Chellaston History Group.

JAMES STEVENS-GREASLEY/GRESLEY

1829/30 - 1908

James Gresley. Watercolour portrait by Benjamin Heald, a contemporary Nottingham artist circa 1865.
Nottingham City Museums & Galleries

JAMES STEVENS-GREASLEY/GRESLEY

1829/30 - 1908

The earliest known artist in the talented Gresley family was James, who was born at Sandiacre, Derbyshire and baptised 23 May 1830 at St. Giles parish church, Sandiacre. He was the youngest of a family of eleven children born to Thomas Greasley and Mary Stevens, who were married at the parish church of All Saints, Ockbrook in 1808.

St.Giles Church Sandiacre, Early illustration by unknown artist
Derbyshire Record Office D4841/25/2

We have no knowledge of any inherited flair for painting, but as both Thomas and Mary were lace makers, it is possible that they created their own designs and the youthful James may have spent time observing his parents at their skilled work. Lace-making was a specialised craft in the Nottingham area where much of it was manufactured as a cottage industry.

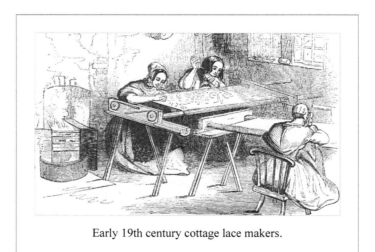

Early 19th century cottage lace makers.

Of James Greasley's early life and training there is no known record but we must assume that he showed a special talent for art at an early age and this gift may have been encouraged by an enthusiastic school master. Many children in the early Victorian era received little or no education at all and worked during their tender years in factories, on the land, or were sent into domestic service. However, we know that James could read and write, so he must have attended a place of learning somewhere. Quite possibly this could have been at a Dame school in the village of Sandiacre.

One wonders if there was a possible relationship between Mary Stevens (mother of James) and the well-known talented architect Henry Isaac Stevens, whose father Isaac Nehemiah lived for a time in Ockbrook. If this relationship could be proven, the gift of artistry could well have been inherited by James through the Stevens family. Is this the reason why at the age of twenty four, he decided to include the name Stevens in his surname? Although Thomas Greasley died at Radford, Nottingham at the age of eighty three, both he and his wife Mary are buried in Sandiacre churchyard, where a handsome slate stone marks their grave.

Handsome slate headstone in Sandiacre Churchyard
marks the grave of Thomas & Mary Greasley.

At the beginning of the nineteenth century, Sandiacre would have been a small rural community and we can imagine the boy James roaming about the countryside, noting with an artist's observant eye all the beauties of nature; the varying cloud formations, reflections on river and stream, water gushing over rocks and pebbles and tree shapes with their seasonal changing colours. Maybe, during those early formative years, James used his sketchbook or slate to illustrate the country landscapes, which he beheld. Like other earlier artists, it seems probable that James Greasley initially taught himself to draw by the time-honoured method of copying prints. Indeed, we read that this is the way in which the famous artist Joseph Wright of Derby developed his early drawing skills.

At the age of seventeen, James was sent to London to be apprenticed to George Johann Scharf, the engraver, under whose influence he became a skilful draughtsman, attaining considerable proficiency. One wonders how a young boy from a relatively poor family could have gained an apprenticeship with a well known engraver and artist like George Scharf. Could this have been the influence of the architect Henry Isaac Stevens who may have been a relative of his mother Mary Stevens? Painting, however, was his real bent and he forsook his engraving for the call of the art studio. It is a remarkable fact that his early training and skill as an engraver was never lost and those who are familiar with his work will have noted how precise he always was in his outlines and how careful in regard to those details which often escape the average painter. Yet while he was meticulous in this respect, he never overdid it and his pastorals rank today among the best of their kind. George Johann Scharf was born in Mainburg, Germany in 1788, son of a tradesman and he studied in Munich, Paris and Antwerp. He moved to London in 1816 where he practised as an artist and engraver. He is principally known as one of the earlier lithographic draughtsmen. Between 1817-1850 he exhibited paintings at the Royal Academy. Charles Darwin commissioned Scharf for a series of illustrations of fossil bones from South America. Scharf also worked as a miniature painter and drawing master. He died in 1860 aged 72 and is best remembered for his paintings "Parliament at Westminster", "Westminster Elections of 1818" and "The Lord Mayor's Feast". The meticulous detail in his painting "Representation of the Election of Members in Covent Garden 1818", which hangs in the Royal Collection at Windsor Castle is worthy of note. A large number of his drawings and watercolours are in the British Museum.

We know that in 1850, at the early age of twenty one years, James Greasley held the post of drawing master at the "Mechanic's Institution" on Mansfield Road in Nottingham where he had one of his pictures exhibited entitled "Yew Tree, Sandiacre Church". This exhibition of Arts, Manufactures, Curiosity and Practical Science was held in the Mechanic's Hall, Nottingham in 1850. At this time he left his home in Sandiacre and two years later we find him residing in Manvers Street, New Sneinton, Nottingham.

On August 5th 1854, at the age of twenty four, James Greasley was married to nineteen-year-old Betsy Maria Smith at Sneinton Parish Church in Nottingham. It is interesting to note that Betsy's parents were also lace-makers. At the time of his marriage to Betsy, James appears to have changed the spelling of his surname to Gresley. Around this time he also added his mother's maiden name of Stevens and he became James Stevens-Gresley and not, Stephen, as many people now believe. From then on, he signed all his paintings J.S.Gresley but the will he made in 1875 was simply signed James Gresley. However, his death certificate dated 1908 states James Stevens Gresley.

The newly married young couple very soon left Nottingham and moved to Derby, where James had obtained the post of drawing master at Derby's first School of Art. This first school, established in the year 1853 was at the bottom of St. Peters Street, Derby at the rear of Joseph Strutt's town house. This house stood where the present day H.S.B.C. Bank is now situated beside Thorntree Lane. Augustus Oakley Deacon was the Art School's master and James was appointed as his assistant. There may have been an earlier connection between Deacon and Gresley as we find that for a period Deacon resided in Ockbrook where the family of James' mother lived. At this time, James and Betsy were living in Abbey Street, Derby, where in 1855 their first child Frank was born. We may read the following extract in Glover's Directory of 1858 referring to Derby's first School of Art:

The object of this institution is drawing of the order and on the most approved principles and to render such instruction accessible to all classes of the public. Mr. Augustus Oakley Deacon is the master and Mr. Gresley assistant master.

During this period 350 pupils were attending the Art School, so the two masters made requests for a new and larger School of Art in Derby. Eventually these two enthusiastic masters managed to convince the authorities that a new Art School was needed and the year 1876 saw the building of the large Victorian Gothic "Central School of Art" in Green Lane Derby.

The following extract is taken from "The Derbyshire Advertiser" of August 1876 and gives the following description: -

The foundation stone of the new building was laid by the Right Hon.
The Baroness Burdett-Coutts. A procession consisting of the Mayor,
members of the Corporation, students and friends of the Institution,
with persons of influence and position in the town proceeded from the
Guildhall en route for the school site on Green Hill. During the parade,
the rain fell in torrents causing the progress of the cortege to be delayed
for a quarter of an hour. The procession was headed by a detachment of
the Police under the command of Colonel Delaconbe and retinue of
javelin men! Although the rain still poured down, things were enlivened
by the strains of the Silver Band. At half past one, Lady Burdett-Coutts
accompanied by her attendant Mrs Browne, was conducted to a carpeted
dais. Her Ladyship was dressed in a handsome blue corded silk dress
and train trimmed with costly lace and a cream coloured cashmere shawl,
fastened at the waist with a plain gold broach, handsomely chased with
her Ladyship's arms. Her bonnet was of cream coloured silk and lace,
trimmed with the hawthorn leaf and primrose flowers, the whole
presenting a most tasteful appearance.

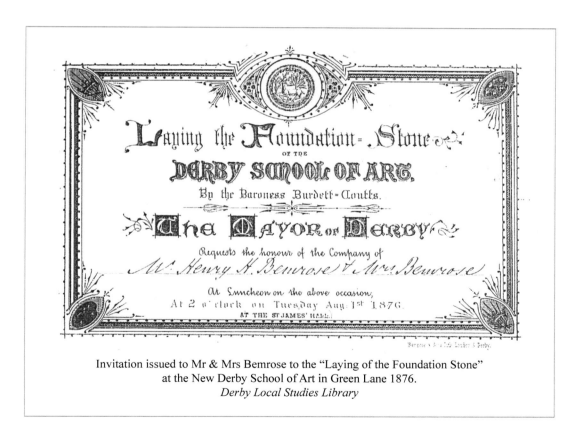

Invitation issued to Mr & Mrs Bemrose to the "Laying of the Foundation Stone"
at the New Derby School of Art in Green Lane 1876.
Derby Local Studies Library

Augustus Oakley Deacon, and James Stevens Gresley were the joint founders of this new Art School where Gresley was the assistant master but in typical Victorian fashion, only the names of the gentry and important personalities were recorded in the newspaper. The poor insignificant drawing masters, who were the instigators of the building, received no mention in the press report although the headmaster of the new School of Art Mr Thomas Simmonds was. Unfortunately, the foundation stone which was laid in 1876 is no longer evident.

Victorian Gothic "Central School of Art", Green Lane, Derby. Built 1876.

It is interesting to note that James held free evening classes to encourage interested pupils; an innovation almost entirely unknown in Victorian times. At some time during this period James was employed by Repton School as a drawing master in the art department. While he was teaching at the School of Art in Derby, he instructed and took under his wing William Henry James Boot of Nottingham, who in later years became a well-known local artist. A deep personal friendship sprang up between Boot and his old tutor. Boot's early work, distinctive in its way, shows clearly the great influence which Gresley exercised over him.

The family lived at several addresses in Derby and after leaving Abbey Street in 1857 they moved to "Normanton Villa" and then to Crompton Street, where they lived for a number of years. During this time, in January 1868, James's children Frank, Clarence, Rosalind, Alice and Percy Richard were all baptised at St. Andrew's Church, which was situated on London Road in Derby, on the site now occupied by St.Andrew's House. The two youngest children of James and Betsy, Marguerite and Emma were not yet born and sadly, Marguerite died as an infant. Another move in 1876 took the Gresley family to "Ivy House" in Charnwood Street, when the houses there were quite new. We find that on an old map of Derby, Charnwood Street was developed from a small byway called "Lovers' Lane". From Charnwood Street the family soon moved to nearby Hartington Street where we find them in 1878. They then made a complete change and took a house in Wilne Lane, Draycott called "Derwent Cottage", before moving to Borrowash in 1882 to 1884. For the painting of portraits, James had a studio in Victoria Street, Derby.

Ivy House in Charnwood St, Derby.
James Gresley's home in 1876.

"Derwent Cottage", Wilne Lane, Draycott. The Gresley family Lived here circa 1880.

During the year 1863, an excellent book was published called "Days in Derbyshire" written by Dr. Spencer T.Hall, containing some very fine wood engravings created by James. The author in his preface thanks *Mr.J.S.Gresley of Derby for his exquisite drawings*. One of the engravings shows a rambler in the Peak District and I feel this possibly could be a self-portrait of James himself, as the man appears to be carrying a sketch book and has an easel strapped to his back. There are fourteen Gresley engravings in the book, all finely drawn and illustrating local places such as Repton, Derby Lunatic Asylum, Haddon Hall, Dale Abbey and Derby Grammar School, to name but a few. This book has long been out of print, but can be fully recommended, both for the content and the charming topographical illustrations. A copy is held by Derby Local Studies Library. James Gresley often used a monogram to sign these engravings. The skill gained during his early training as an engraver under George Scharf in London, shines through this work.

During the autumn of 1866, an Art and Industrial Exhibition was held in the Corn Exchange, Derby in aid of the building funds for the Churches of St. Andrew and St. James. It is interesting to note that a landscape painted by James entitled "On the Trent near Barrow" was displayed and sold for £15 15s 0d, a considerable sum of money at that time.

Two of James's children inherited the talent for painting. Frank, the eldest, became the noted local landscape artist but his gifted sister Alice is not so well remembered. Being a girl, her talent was probably not encouraged to the same degree. In those Victorian times, middle class girls were not expected to work for a living, so Alice merely painted her pictures for a pastime. However, occasionally her watercolours are still to be found in sale-rooms or private collections. It is a pity that Alice had no opportunity to develop her natural skills and technique to become as well known as her brother Frank.

James' son Percy Richard, born in 1865, joined the Navy at the early age of fourteen as a midshipman. He eventually emigrated to Australia and married Susannah Ostler in 1888. His great grandson Stuart Gresley, who resides in New South Wales, has kindly sent me a photograph of an early oil painting by James. This painting depicts an elegant lady dressed in early Victorian clothes who is reputed to be "Aunt Mary". She must have been either James' sister or his mother and the portrait, measuring thirty by twenty five inches must have been one of his earliest attempts at portraiture. I also received photographs of two rural landscapes, both signed and dated 1883. One shows the river Wharfe in Yorkshire and the other is a large country cottage, which Stuart Gresley tells me is reputed to have been the old family home at Sandiacre.

Eventually, James, with his wife and younger children, left Derby and went to live in Yorkshire at Bolton Abbey, where he found inspiration in the atmospheric and sometimes dramatic scenery of the Yorkshire Dales. He produced several landscapes of Bolton Abbey itself, which appears to have been one of his favourite subjects.

During the late eighteenth century and early nineteenth century, a Welsh tour had become almost obligatory for any aspiring landscape artist, the Welsh castles being one of the most popular subjects. James painted "Conway Castle" in watercolours, showing a grey stormy sky with a mass of birds being tossed about in the wind, smoke curling from cottage chimneys and fisher-folk in the foreground busily filling their baskets.

The splendid countryside of North Wales is well represented among James' landscape paintings. They are mainly watercolours but some are exquisitely executed in oils. A magnificent oil on canvas may be seen in Derby Art Gallery and is entitled "Swallow Falls". The use of heavily applied white paint in the cascading torrent gives emphasis to the strength and powerful force of the water gushing onto the boulders below. The small thick dabs of paint give an excellent impression of light on the sparkling water. So realistic is the painting one feels one can almost hear the roar of the mighty waterfall. Another excellent and very large oil painting called "Prospect of Derby" also hangs in Derby Art Gallery. This important picture painted from Mount Carmel on Burton Road is full of local interest, depicting the imposing tower of All Saints parish church and the old Shot Tower in the Morledge, which dominated the local landscape from 1808-1931. The picture shows the presence of many other church towers and spires in the background, which give the composition an extra dimension of appeal. Some of these spires and towers have now sadly disappeared. The figures and animals in the rural green foreground give added interest, creating an atmosphere of timeless, magical summer days.

J.S. Gresley in his later years. Sketched by Gresley Shreeve who was a member of the family.
Derby Museums & Art Gallery

After a time, James decided to leave Bolton Abbey and moved to Ilkley, the spa town on the Yorkshire moors. This move was probably made to enable him to find more scope in discovering the beautiful views, which he needed to portray in his work. He took his images from his observation of Yorkshire life and people.

James' last and final move in 1897 was to Wakefield, where he died in October 1908 aged seventy-seven years, while residing at 32 Southgate. He had been in failing health for some time and died of senile decay. His obituary in the Wakefield Express stated:

> *Latterly the enfeebled health of Mr Gresley whose signature on a watercolour*
> *might be accepted as the hallmark of high merit, compelled him to lay aside*
> *his brush and forsake the art he had loved so well. It is a remarkable fact that*
> *his early training as an engraver was never lost upon him and those who are at*
> *all familiar with his work will remember how precise he always was in his*
> *outlines, and how careful he was in regard to those details which escape the*
> *average painter. Yet while he was punctilious in this respect, he never overdid*
> *it, and his pastorals rank among the best of their kind.*

His daughter Alice, who had remained a spinster, had already died in 1903 at the age of forty. His wife Betsy Maria continued to live in Wakefield with their daughter Rosalind until her death in 1926 at the age of ninety. Rosalind lived to be 77 and died in 1936 while residing at 92 York Street. They are all four buried in Wakefield City Cemetery. Sadly, no memorial stone marks their grave.

It was said that James would never submit any of his work to the big galleries. The many art critics whom he numbered among his friends always declared that his dislike for notability was a reason for his fame being less wide, though he was generally accepted at the chief provincial exhibitions. At Birmingham in particular, he always sold well. However, he did have pictures accepted at London galleries from 1866, including the R.B.A., (Royal Society of British Artists) the R.I. (Royal Institute of Painters in Water Colours), once at the S.S. (Society of British Artists) and again at the N.W.S. (New Watercolour Society).

James Stevens Gresley was a typical Victorian artist and although he might not be one of the major names in Victorian art, his pictures of 19th century life are both appealing and consistently eye-catching. Although he was born in the Pre-Raphaelite era, he did not follow this style, preferring art in the more traditional vein. We need to remember James as an artist who became a master of his craft without a great deal of training and when we consider this, his achievement was quite staggering. Through the ensuing years, his charming landscapes have given much pleasure to countless people.

James Stevens Gresley, circa 1879.
This illustration of J.S. Gresley has been sent from Australia.
Note the artist's sketch-book, smock & old hat!

Percy Richard Gresley aged 14 years.
Midshipman. Son of James who
eventually emigrated to Australia
and was the grandfather of
Stuart Gresley who provided
these photographs.

Rosalind Gresley aged 19 years.
She died unmarried at Wakefield in
1936 at the age of seventy-seven.

Alice Gresley aged 16 years.
Alice became a talented artist
in her own right and died in
1903 aged forty.

Emma Gresley aged 10 years
daughter of James. Sadly, she died
while still a child. Note that all three
girls appear to be similarly dressed.
Another daughter, Marguerite,
died as an infant.

Paintings of James Stevens Gresley

Reputed to be the family home of the Gresleys at Sandiacre. Signed and dated 1883.

Prospect of Derby from Burton Road. Note the cornfields, cattle grazing & people enjoying the
countryside. Also observe the tower of "All Saints" Church. Oil on canvas. 1861
Derby Museums & Art Gallery

Conway Castle with fisher-folk in the foreground.

Penmachno Mill, North Wales. Signed and dated 1901.

"Swallow Falls" North Wales. Dramatic landscape showing a spectacular vista of the falls.
Derby Museums & Art Gallery

Tintern Abbey, Monmouthshire.

Aunt Mary
Painted by James Gresley
Oil on canvas, unsigned.
A family portrait from Australia,
reputed to be either
James Gresley's mother
or his sister Mary.

"Dick"
James Gresley's dog.
Oil on canvas.

"Swallow Falls" Betws-y-Coed, with female figures on the rocks. Signed and dated 1893.

The Manifold Valley from Fishers Cave. Dated 1893
Derby Museums & Art Gallery

Blackberry Picking at Dale Abbey
Derby Museums & Art Gallery

Fairy Glen
Betws-y-Coed
1882
Derby Museums & Art Gallery

Engravings created by James Stevens Gresley for the book 'Days in Derbyshire' by Dr. Spencer T Hall.
Published in 1863.

A Peak Tourist.
This could well be a self portrait of J.S.Gresley. Note the sketch book,
the easel strapped to his back and the artist's hat.

The Derby Grammar Schools, St. Helen's House

The Derby County Lunatic Asylum, Mickleover.

Repton Church and the Archway.

Dale Abbey. The Window Arch.

Haddon Hall. Dorothy Vernon Steps.

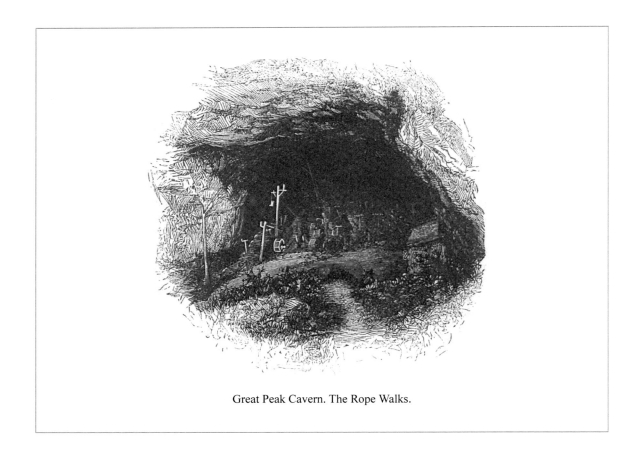

Great Peak Cavern. The Rope Walks.

Anchor Church. An Anchorite Hermitage.

Bonsall Cross.

Intricate engraving of Foxglove and Fern.

Accordion Player.
A half-witted rustic who made music and danced
in the streets of Matlock.

Effigy in 13th century Scarcliffe Church,
of a lady holding a child. The lady is probably
one of the family of Frenchville.

Dethick Church.
Associated with
the Babbington family.

Haddon Hall.
The Eagle Tower.

FRANK GRESLEY

1855 - 1936

Portrait of Frank. Painted by his son Harold. Oil on canvas.
Derby Museums & Art Gallery

FRANK GRESLEY

1855 - 1936

On 8th May 1855, when Queen Victoria was only thirty six years old, Lord Palmerston was the Prime Minister and the British Army was fighting bloody battles in the Crimea, Frank Gresley was born in Abbey Street, in the newly built up centre of Derby. He was the eldest child of James and Betsy Maria Gresley, who had come to live in Derby soon after their marriage in Nottingham in 1854.

Very little is known about Frank's early life and training but he would almost certainly have been tutored by his artist father. More than likely he would have been a pupil at the Derby School of Art in St Peter's Street, where his father was a drawing master. A great deal of young Frank's time must have been spent in an artistic atmosphere, watching his father at work on his traditional images of rural life. He may have accompanied him on jaunts around the local countryside, through picturesque villages, the beautiful Derbyshire Dales and the lush river valleys of the Trent, the Derwent and the Dove. He would have taken note of the ever-changing play of colours in the varying skies of sunrise and sunset, scudding clouds and the effects of light. Scenes such as these were typical of J.S. Gresley's work. In this way, the young Frank would have developed an awareness of landscape, studying plants and flowers, exploring streams and rivers and observing local bird life.

At the age of twenty-one, in the year 1876, Frank married twenty-year-old Harriet Fearn at St.Peter's Church in Derby. Harriet was the only daughter of George Fearn, a very well known publican in Derby, where he and his sons between them ran seventeen pubs from 1860/1900! When Harriet married Frank Gresley, her father was licensee of "The Corporation Hotel" in the old Derby Cattle Market.

"Elm Tree Cottage", Bakehouse Lane, Ockbrook.

Like his father before him, Frank lived at various addresses, which included Byron Street in Derby where his eldest son Cuthbert was born in 1877. From Byron Street, the family moved to the rural village of Ockbrook, where they lived at Elm Tree Cottage in Bakehouse Lane. To help Harriet in the house, a fourteen-year-old servant girl was employed named Bertha Peat, to help with cooking, housework and childminding. The next move was to Borrowash, where surprisingly, Frank became the landlord of the "Noah's Ark" on Nottingham Road and in 1887 we find yet another pub as the Gresley residence. This time, the "Queens Head" in Ockbrook! As Harriet had been born and brought up in a hotel she would have gleaned a great deal of knowledge about the management of these places and this may have been the reason why Frank decided to become a publican. The Gresley family was always very poor and Frank would no doubt have been trying to earn a little extra much-needed money to supplement the meagre income from his paintings. By this time, Frank and Harriet had five children: Rosalind, called Rose, Cuthbert, Noel, Horace and Mabel. Their youngest child, Harold, was born in 1892 at 2 Windmill Hill Lane in Derby.

"Noah's Ark", Borrowash.

"Queen's Head", Ockbrook.

The next and final place of residence for Frank's family was "Crow Tree House" in School Lane, at Chellaston. This was in 1892 and there it was that Frank stayed for the rest of his life. School Lane in Chellaston is located in the oldest part of the village and "Crow Tree House" is situated next door to the school which had been built in 1876. Frank soon became a well-known and familiar character among the villagers and observed their activities, many of which can be noted in his paintings, such as the drover with his herd of cattle or flock of sheep, country housewives gossiping on doorsteps, children at play and farm carts trundling along the lanes. Thus did Frank Gresley take his inspiration predominantly from everyday subjects and sentimentally idealised images of Victorian life. His traditional portrayals of a rural lifestyle make the name Frank Gresley synonymous with scenes of rustic life and in today's hectic and often chaotic atmosphere with the continual noise of traffic, and the vulgarity of garish colours, to relax and contemplate a Frank Gresley landscape takes one back to the days of peace and tranquillity. His studios however were situated in Victoria Street and All Saints Chambers, situated in Iron Gate, Derby.

He painted prolifically and wandered all around the Trent Valley searching for the most suitable scenes to develop into his landscape paintings. One of the older residents of Chellaston, the late Miss Betty Forman, now sadly deceased, remembered Frank Gresley quite vividly from her childhood days. She then lived at "The Elms", a farmhouse which stood right opposite the Gresley home and she told us that Frank had a white moustache and a trimmed goatee beard. Each day he would set forth wearing a slouched hat, with his easel, paints and sketch book under one arm, a raincoat over the other and his little dog "Pop" on a lead. He walked miles and miles to paint his pictures. Of course, he was much too poor to afford a pony and trap, car, or even a bicycle, so walking was the order of the day. He could have taken a train from Chellaston station to Melbourne and after 1920, he may have boarded a "Higgs and Waller" bus to help him reach the local beauty spots. Most of the charming villages of the Trent Valley are depicted on Frank's paintings, including Swarkestone, Aston-on-Trent, Weston-on-Trent, Stanton-by-Bridge, Barrow-on-Trent, Ticknall, Twyford, Repton, King's Mills, and of course, his own village of Chellaston. Apparently, every morning, before starting off on his painting jaunts, Frank would go over to the farm with Pop and his can, for milk. On wet, muddy mornings Frank would say, "Now Pop, don't go making any pansies on Mrs Forman's nice clean floor". Who but an artist would compare a little dog's foot prints to pansies!

We must remember that Frank had a growing family to support and as she grew older, his wife Harriet became a chronic invalid, confined to a wheelchair. During the 19th Century, painting as a profession was neither lucrative nor regarded highly, other than for a few major artists.

At that time, the Chellaston locals didn't rate Frank Gresley's pictures very highly and they were known as, "Frank Gresley's greenery-yallery pot boilers!" According to the well-known artist Stanley Spencer, pot boilers keep the wolves from the door and there were certainly often wolves baying at Frank Gresley's door. This is why his output had to be so prolific. Despite all this, it was said of Frank Gresley that he immortalised the river Trent and the surrounding area with his paintings. We are led to believe that royalty purchased one of his pictures entitled "The Silver Trent". Certainly, the name Frank Gresley is synonymous with the Trent Valley scenery. Like his father before him, Frank also loved to paint the wild scenery of North Wales with its rushing torrents, mountains and beautiful valleys and streams. He may, of course, at times have used his father's sketchbook to portray this magnificent scenery, taking his inspiration predominantly from everyday subjects.

Two of Frank's sons, Horace and Noel, volunteered to fight in the Boer War, having been selected for the Imperial Yeomanry in February 1901. The Derby Mercury tells us that

Horace Gresley was a member of Chellaston Church choir and, together with Selwyn Meakin, was given a hearty send off to the Boer War by his fellow choristers. They were both presented with a knapsack, bible and an Ancient and Modern hymn book with tunes and a pipe and case. Before the company dispersed, Auld Lang Syne was sung very heartily by all.

When the First World War came, all four of Frank Gresley's sons took part and the following is an extract from a letter written by Frank to his brother Percy in Australia in 1916:

> As you know, I'm quite alone now. It seems very strange and a century
> while waiting here and wondering day by day what is happening. I really
> don't know what I should do if anything happened to Harold. I have spent
> the latter part of my life for him and hoping, as I may say to live part of it
> over again, when he gets finally going in his career. He was still at school
> when the war broke out. He is very clever and can draw or paint anything.
> Portraits, landscapes - anything. I am very glad he managed to paint a
> wonderfully good portrait of his mother before she died.
> He was only nineteen when he did it.
>
> He has been to the Dardenelles and got damaged there but soon got well again
> and is now in France in the 1st Battalion Royal Fusiliers. He got his stripe a
> few days ago and is now Lance Corporal. He could have had promotion over
> twelve months ago but would not take it until he was on active service.
>
> Noel is in hospital in France but is progressing well and may get a few days
> leave when he comes out of hospital. He has been out twelve months in the
> R.F.A. I understand his horse fell into a shell hole and rolled over him but I
> do not think there were any bones broken.
>
> Horace is in Salonica. He was called up when war broke out as he was on
> the Reserve having been in the army for a good many years after the Boer War.

By the end of the First World War, the quiet rural life that Frank had enjoyed and painted had all but disappeared, but he continued to paint traditional landscapes of his beloved Trent Valley, which he had immortalised.

In his later years Frank Gresley was known as "The Grand Old Man of Chellaston", being the oldest male resident in the village. He died in hospital in 1936 at the age of eighty-two and is buried in Chellaston churchyard, but unfortunately, there is no stone to mark his grave. An interesting fact to note is that the funeral arrangements were carried out by Crocker Bros. who are still in business in Chellaston and the service was conducted by the Rev. Plemming, whom many Chellaston people still remember with affection. Harriet Gresley had died in on 2nd April 1914, twenty-two years before her husband.

Frank Gresley may not be one of the major names in Victorian art, but his landscape paintings are now much sought after in art shops and salerooms nationwide. It is sad to think how he struggled with his work to make ends meet and provide for his family. Now, almost seventy years after his death, his pictures fetch a price that would have been untold wealth to the poor hard working artist.

The paintings executed by Frank followed very much the style and techniques of his father's work and this is very evident in his landscapes. For much of the 20th century the English neglected and despised the art of the 19th century. Today however, a complete reassessment has taken place, and at last, it is possible to see the pictures of the Victorian age as part of the overall history of English art. Watercolourists like Frank Gresley reflected the fashion for cluttered interiors and cottage gardens full of old fashioned species. These paintings during the 20th century were not being sought after or collected, but were cast on one side as too sentimentally idealised images of Victorian rural life. The work of the lesser known Victorian artists has once again found its place in society and is a clear reflection of the tastes, aspirations and prejudices of the Victorian era.

Frank Gresley's pictures are of a conventional composition, showing plenty of trees and foliage, which were often depicted with warm autumnal colours. They show impressive skies with varying cloud formations and usually a few Victorian figures or animals to give interest to the scene. Like his father, he loved to paint views showing overpowering rocks with gushing torrents as well as the peaceful scenes of South Derbyshire. Frank Gresley will always be remembered as the artist who gave the river Trent and its environs an eternal timelessness. His fine portrayals of the area give the viewer a feeling of the tranquillity and peace of a bygone age, which seems lost to us now when the countryside is so quickly being eaten up by the age of industry.

"Crow Tree House", School Lane, Chellaston.
Originally the front door was between the two windows.

Selection of Paintings by Frank Gresley

The River Trent at Swarkestone, dated 1894.
Note the effect of the light to emphasise the gentle charm of the scene.

Harvest time near Ingleby, portraying traditional images of rural life. Dated 1894.

Swarkestone Bowling Pavilion & Green
showing Frank's inoffensive style and tranquil composition.

The Ferry, Barrow on Trent.

A peaceful scene of autumn.
Believed to be Chellaston with the church tower in the background.
Derby Museums & Art Gallery

Markeaton Brook. An autumnal scene with a mellow quality.
Note Frank's observation of trees and foliage at which he excelled.

Woman washing clothes by a stream.
Note the effect of light and the solitary
cow to give a touch of interest.

Ingleby Lane, Ingleby.
A competent and pleasing painting
with charming rustic appeal.

Swarkestone Road, Chellaston, showing the 'Rose & Crown Inn'.

The High Street and St. Peter's Church, Chellaston.

Maybe a distant view of Chellaston village.

Chellaston church and 'The Yews' farmhouse. Painted from the Flatts
showing the High Street before the building of any houses.

CUTHBERT GRESLEY

1877-1962/3

Cuthbert Gresley, taken at the 'Traveller's Joy Café'.
"Royal Crown Derby" by John Twitchett & Betty Bailey

CUTHBERT GRESLEY

1877-1962/3

In the winter of 1877, with the weather probably iron-cold, roof tops glittering with frost and people scurrying along the streets of Derby with coat collars turned up against the intense chill of an English winter, Frank Gresley's eldest son Cuthbert was born on 17 December. At this time, the family was living in Byron Street at Normanton-by-Derby but Cuthbert was baptised on 20 February 1878 at St Andrew's Church in Derby.

Some time during the following few years, Frank and Harriet Gresley with their two young children, Rosalind and Cuthbert, moved to the charming village of Ockbrook, where two more sons, Noel and Horace, were born. Although very young and poor at this time, the Gresleys were still able to employ the young girl, Bertha Peat, to help as a servant. When the Gresley family moved to nearby Borrowash the three young sons attended the village school but the eldest child, Rosalind, is thought to have been educated at a small private school in Ockbrook village.

Like his father and grandfather before him, Cuthbert became an extremely gifted artist and must have shown great promise at a very early age. There is no doubt that during those formative years he would have been tutored and encouraged by his father, Frank, and we must remember that grandfather James was still painting prolifically at this time. The newly built Derby School of Art in Green Lane was flourishing during the late Victorian era and it was there that Cuthbert continued to pursue his interest in drawing and painting.

From his early youth, Cuthbert was always an enthusiastic sportsman, taking much interest in football. At one time, for a period of four years, he captained an old Derby football team called "Derby Fosse" F.C., playing centre forward and he played in trial games with celebrities such as Steve Bloomer. After moving with the family to Chellaston in about 1892, he became captain of the Chellaston village football team. In his last season with this club, in 1912-13, it won all its twenty-six matches plus the League Cup Final at the Baseball Ground, Derby, without conceding a single goal.

At the age of eighteen in 1893, Cuthbert Gresley started his artistic career. Although the Gresley landscape painters James, Frank and later, Harold, are renowned for their charming watercolour landscapes, Cuthbert's work on porcelain took on a different art form, being mainly floral decoration, very finely executed and with a riot of nature's colours. His deep love and appreciation of all flowers, both wild and cultivated, was reflected in his work. Leaving the School of Art, he was accepted as an apprentice artist with the Royal Crown Derby China Company on Osmaston Road, in Derby and was trained to paint on porcelain by the already well-known china painter, John Porter Wale. At first, he received no wages at all but after a while he was given the princely sum of half a crown a week, this eventually rising to four shillings!

Other well-known china painters who were trained at that time became Cuthbert's close friends, included Robert Barratt, William Mosely, George Jessop and W.E.J. (Billy) Dean. Cuthbert's work at this time was greatly influenced by the colourful flowers and exotic birds painted by Charles Harris. Collectors world-wide now avidly seek the work of all these Royal Crown Derby artists. After working for some years on 'piece-work', Cuthbert Gresley became one of the company's best known artists and his beautifully decorated china travelled the world.

On 18th October 1905, a marriage took place at St.James' Church, Derby, between Emily May Glover and Cuthbert Gresley. At the time of their wedding, the couple were both living in Ladygrove Cottages on the Osmaston Road. These houses, built in 1878 and still standing, form a terrace at the side of the china factory and were built by Edward Phillips to accommodate his workers. Perhaps Cuthbert was a lodger at the home of Mrs Glover, a widow, and her daughter Emily. As Cuthbert's home was in Chellaston, he would have had a long five-mile journey to Derby and back each day and would have found it more convenient to board at Mrs Glover's house.

In those elegant and peaceful pre-First World War days, the English aristocracy was much influenced by the graceful charm of Queen Alexandra, who led the way in fashion and home decoration. A new lifestyle was developed in contrast to the grim severity of the Victorian years and people became more relaxed, carefree and pleasure loving. The eleventh Duke of Bedford, named Herbrand, was no exception to this life of ease and luxury and for the use and delight of his guests he ordered a quantity of Royal Crown Derby china for use on his private yacht. He needed a breakfast service, tea service, coffee service and six mocha coffee cups and saucers. Decoration of this very important order was assigned to Cuthbert and he exquisitely decorated it with garlands of roses. This china much reflected the style and charm of the popular Queen Alexandra. The centre of each plate bears the Bedford family crest. Other important services were painted by Cuthbert Gresley, one of which was presented to the young Princess May for her marriage to Prince George, the Duke of York, afterwards King George V. At a much later date King George VI was also presented with a Royal Crown Derby Gresley-painted service and yet another example of his work from this time went to the royal family of Tibet.

During the year 1906, the wealthy American Judge Elbert H. Gary ordered a quantity of decorative Crown Derby table ware, comprising more than 400 pieces. This service was commissioned through the famous Tiffany Jewellers of New York. Several of the Crown Derby painters, including Cuthbert Gresley, contributed their skills to create the very ornate design of this unique porcelain. This was the most important collection of china ever to leave the Royal Crown Derby factory.

The artist's clear skill in the delicate colouring of his floral painting can bring to life a simple wild flower and the light cheerful palette he used gave depth of colour to the various blooms. The daintiness of a rose-head, forget-me-nots or a tiny fragile leaf became realistic under the creative brush of such a talented artist.

As we have seen, Cuthbert was mostly known for his studies of flowers and birds, but he also decorated many cabinet plates, bowls and vases with landscapes and country houses. Chatsworth House is featured on a Talbot shaped plate showing a view of the north front, with the impressive stone bridge in the foreground. Other pieces show views of well-known beauty spots such as Loch Katrine and Aberfoyle. The Derbyshire Peak District was also a favourite subject for Cuthbert's work and we find ceramic pieces painted with scenes of High Tor, Matlock and Dovedale.

Although Cuthbert Gresley painted landscapes of Scotland, Northern England and Wales, much of this work was taken from "Black's Illustrated Railway Guide" rather than direct observation. It is very doubtful if Cuthbert ever visited Scotland or Wales at all. He may also have used his father Frank's sketchbook.

Many landscape pictures were executed by Cuthbert and these are mostly watercolours depicting picturesque cottages, grassy meadows and river scenes. His pictures are generally of the Trent Valley area around Swarkestone and Ingleby. He rented two rooms at a farm in Ingleby Lane, near the river, to use as his studio and this farmhouse was later converted by the owner to become the well-known and popular "John Thompson Inn".

The early years of Cuthbert's married life were spent at Shelton Lock, the community just north of Chellaston. It was here in "Melbourne Villa" on the main Derby Road that his two sons were born, Cuthbert Kenneth (known as Ken) and Harold. Kenneth became the well-known local builder but Harold, who had always been delicate, sadly died at a very young age just prior to his arranged marriage to Alice, a local hairdresser. Locally, in Shelton Lock and Chellaston, Cuthbert was always known as "Cuff". He was a familiar character to be seen daily, cycling up and down the main road to the china factory in Derby on his "sit-up-and-beg" bicycle, wearing a ginger tweed sports jacket and a cap. Through the years, Cuthbert never lost his great interest and enthusiasm for sport, but as be grew older and could no longer play football, he turned his attention to greyhound racing and successfully raced his own dogs at Derby Greyhound Stadium. In twenty-one years he missed only one meeting at the track. He was also a well-known poultry breeder of trap-nested white Leghorns and white Wyandottes.

"Melbourne Villa", Derby Road, Chellaston.

During the mid nineteen-thirties, Cuff Gresley purchased a piece of land at Shelton Lock on which he developed a beautiful garden. He grew a great variety of flowers and shrubs to produce a show of vivid colours, which delighted the passers-by, and the piece of rough ploughed land became like a miniature park and bird sanctuary. There were lawns, paths, a pool with a bridge and huge rocks brought from Whatstandwell. Later, his friend Miss Eucebia Maud Francis made delicious ice cream, which she sold at the garden gate on Sunday afternoons and evenings. If one purchased an ice cream, one was permitted to stroll around the lovely garden at leisure. In this way, Cuthbert was able to weave together two of his great passions – painting and growing flowers. People came from near and far to sample the ice cream, admire Cuthbert's garden and to hear the nightingale! The story told locally is that when the garden was nicely full of the Sunday evening strollers, Cuthbert would disappear behind the trees with his portable gramophone and play a record of the nightingale sweetly trilling his melodious evening song. One way of encouraging custom!

As the lovely garden, plus the nightingale became more popular, Cuthbert decided to expand his business. During the few years just before the outbreak of World War Two, he built a café and shop in the area adjacent to his garden. When the building was completed it was called "The Traveller's Joy" and he and Miss Eucebia Francis managed it. The café was named after the flower Wild Clematis, otherwise known as "Vitalba" or "Traveller's Joy". There was also a thriving vegetable plot, which Cuthbert cultivated himself, producing fresh vegetables for his café. There were three greenhouses, two of them sixty yards long. Miss Francis had always lived at Shelton Lock and was locally known as Sybil. I feel that she deserves a special mention here for her contribution to art. She furnished and decorated the Traveller's Joy to a high and tasteful standard, the restaurant being hung with Gresley paintings and beautified with pieces of Royal Crown Derby china. A grand piano graced the room and this, with a violin, was played for the "Tea Dances" arranged by Sybil for the ladies and gentlemen of the area. There were also small select dances on Saturday evenings, which continued during the early war years but then ceased, as air raid alerts became more frequent.

"Derby Ram" May 1998 vol. 7 no. 2
Derby Local Studies Library

As a young girl, Sybil Francis was employed as a trainee gilder at the Royal Crown Derby factory. Living at Shelton Lock, she knew the Gresley family very well and it was possibly Cuthbert who obtained work for her as a gilder. She was extremely artistic and her special talent lay in designing and executing fine embroidery. An early example of her work can be seen in the exquisite altar frontal in Chellaston village church. She was also a member of the Royal School of Needlework. Sybil would spend her lunch breaks at the factory working at her embroidery and one day one of the chief designers stopped to admire her latest design of exotic birds. He was so impressed with the work that he asked Sybil if the Royal Crown Derby China Company could use the motif. She gave her consent and from this the popular "Olde Avesbury" and "Aves" designs were created and have been used for many years on much porcelain tableware. During 1978, to celebrate the centenary of the opening of the Royal Crown Derby China Factory, the nearby hotel was renamed "The Olde Avesbury". However the building is no longer a hotel, having been incorporated into the Royal Crown Derby Factory complex.

When trade at the "Traveller's Joy" increased, Cuthbert Gresley retired from the china factory after fifty years of working there, and spent the remainder of his life managing the café full-time with Miss Francis. Many people will remember the "Traveller's Joy" in its heyday, when it was noted for its good food, elegant décor and charming cottage-type garden. Many famous people visited the tearoom in those days, including the actress Anna Neagle with her husband, Herbert Wilcox, and the actor Michael Wilding. When approaching his eightieth birthday, Cuthbert was asked how he retained his youthful energy and he replied, "I don't believe in growing old". He was a non-drinker and non-smoker but stated "I have nothing at all against this".

Cuthbert died at the Traveller's Joy Café in 1963 at the age of eighty-seven. After the death of Cuthbert Gresley and the retirement of Sybil Francis, the "Traveller's Joy" was sold and became the locally well-known eating house called "The Golden Pheasant". At a later date, the ownership changed hands again and became the "Beefeater", a popular restaurant for lunch and evening meals. Today however the name "Golden Pheasant" has been re-established but sadly, Cuthbert's beautiful garden is now a car park, the original building has had its heart torn out and no nightingale sings for the Sunday evening ice-cream eaters!

Although almost fifty years have passed by since Cuthbert's death in 1963, his artistic achievements live on in the charming and sensitive art forms he created on Royal Crown Derby china.

Examples of Cuthbert's exquisite work are exhibited in the Royal Crown Derby China Museum and the Derby City Museum.

Cuthbert Gresley, taken at the 'Traveller's Joy Café'.
"Royal Crown Derby" by John Twitchett & Betty Bailey

Selected watercolours & work painted on
Royal Crown Derby China
by Cuthbert Gresley

Chellaston Church about 1920. Note the absence of the lych-gate which was erected
as a memorial to those who lost their lives in World War One.

Bowl of roses on window ledge at 'Travellers Joy Café'.

The Fox Covert at Chellaston
Derby Museums & Art Gallery

Cluster of Wild Flowers
Derby Museums & Art Gallery

Still life, entitled 'Peonies from my Garden'.
This would have been at the 'Traveller's Joy Café' in Shelton Lock, now 'The Golden Pheasant'.

Still life, floral spray
signed and dated 1906

Still life, floral spray
unsigned.

Royal Crown Derby tea cup & saucer dated 1912 from the Duke of Bedford's yacht service,
pattern 8979. Sprays of Roses painted by Cuthbert Gresley (not signed).

Royal Crown Derby plate dated 1905
signed Cuthbert Gresley.

Royal Crown Derby two handled lidded vase painted by Cuthbert. Produced for the Borough of Derby and inscribed on the base "In commemoration of the opening of the Electric Tramways on the 27th July 1904".

Royal Crown Derby Porcelain Company Limited

Royal Crown Derby floral decorated plate by Cuthbert Gresley dated 1900.

Royal Crown Derby plate c.1895 painted with wild roses, signed C. Gresley.

Royal Crown Derby comport signed C. Gresley.

Royal Crown Derby plate dated 1920. The centre, a view of Neidpath Castle in Scotland.
Royal Crown Derby Porcelain Company Limited

Porcelain medallion mounted as a brooch, circa 1920. Signed C. Gresley.

Royal Crown Derby comport. Puce feather scrolls & gilt.
View of Kilburn Castle, Scotland by C. Gresley. Date code 1923.

Royal Crown Derby vase dated 1908,
Painted by Cuthbert Gresley.

HAROLD GRESLEY

1892 - 1967

Harold Gresley in action painting peacefully by a canal on 19th July 1949.
Derby Evening Telegraph

HAROLD GRESLEY

1892 - 1967

The last and youngest member of the Gresley family of artists was Harold, who was born on 9th March 1892 at 2 Windmill Hill Lane, Derby. He was sixteen years younger than his brother Cuthbert.

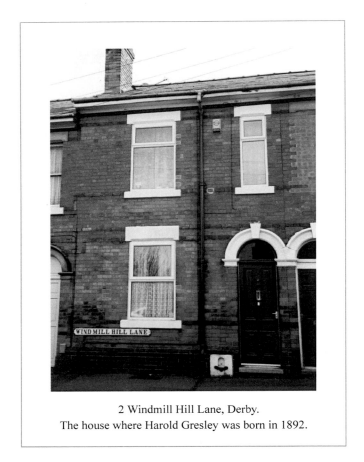

2 Windmill Hill Lane, Derby.
The house where Harold Gresley was born in 1892.

In many ways, Harold carried on the work of his father Frank, and grandfather James, and it would be wrong to place his work on too high a plane in the hierarchy of English artists. However, apart from the famous Wright of Derby and George Turner, there are few local artists whose work is more appreciated by Derbyshire people than the Gresleys' delightful watercolours and portraits. Harold's charming paintings must bring back to many people memories of our beautiful county, especially that part through which the silver Trent still gently flows with placid grace, despite the building of power stations and gravel works! He developed the ability to create sparkling gems by his close observation of nature. Many scenes include water. He embraced the scope water gave for playing with light and reflection. Harold's work can be found in a number of galleries, but above all, in the Derby Art Gallery and in the Goodey Collection also housed in that gallery. There are also many paintings of the limestone country of north Derbyshire and of Snowdonia and the Welsh coast. As a very young child, Harold attended the village school at Chellaston, which is situated next door to "Crow Tree House", the Gresley home in School Lane. His artistic career began in 1912 at the Derby School of Art, the old grey Gothic Victorian building in Green Lane, of which his grandfather James was one of the founders. Later in 1919, after his military service in the Great War, he studied at Nottingham Art School under the direction of the well-known artist Arthur Spooner. From Nottingham, he won gold and silver medallion awards and gained a scholarship to the Royal College of Art in London. At the age of fifteen, Harold entered drawing competitions for children run by the Derby Mercury newspaper. He was very highly commended for a drawing of *"an unfortunate young gentleman in the stocks receiving a shower of dead cats, rotten eggs, carrots, etc, whilst a guard in full armour "kept sentry". The gentleman in the stocks attired not unlike a jester."* Harold won first prize in January 1908, receiving half a sovereign for a drawing of a lion's head, after a sketch by Herbert Dicksee. He won second prize (2 shillings) for an excellent copy of a drawing in "The Studio". Three months later he won a prize with a picture of *"a medieval bass-viol player carrying his instrument in one arm and his volume "Musick" under the other, about to be ushered into the presence of the Mighty Baron and looking about as "sick" as he could"*.

When in 1914, the country took up arms against Germany, Harold Gresley enlisted in the army in August 1915. He took part in the fierce fighting at the Gallipoli landings in the Dardenelles where he was wounded. For his bravery, he was awarded the D.C.M and at this stage he was made a sergeant in the Royal Fusiliers. On leaving the army at the end of the Great War, Harold did not take advantage of his scholarship at the Royal College of Art in London. He worked for a short time at the Royal Crown Derby China Factory until in 1924 he gained the post of assistant Art Master at Repton School and he remained in that position for the rest of his working life, which was another thirty years.

On August 26th 1920, when he was twenty eight, Harold married a lovely young lady named Clara Hitchin and the ceremony took place at St. Chad's Church, Derby. The young couple made their home with father Frank in School Lane, Chellaston, and stayed there for the rest of their lives. After Harold's death, Clara stayed on alone as long as she could manage, eventually deciding to move into a residential home, where she died.

In 1925-26, many excellent townscapes were painted by Harold, most of them forming part of the "Goodey Collection", which was donated by Alfred Goodey to Derby Art Gallery, where they have been since 1936. These pictures depict the town as it was in pre Second World War days. We see the "Old Dolphin" and the "Bull's Head" on the corners of Full Street with the Power Station just being built in the background. Most of this has now been swept away and with the road-widening the old "Bulls Head" also disappeared. The wrought iron inn sign at the "Bull's Head", fashioned by Robert Bakewell, is thankfully, now in safe hands at the Derby Museum and the "Old Dolphin" still stands. Other pictures in this series show St. Michael's Lane, Green Lane, Full Street with an old inn called the "Horse and Trumpet", and St. Helen's Street. Perhaps the most interesting picture was painted from the Cattle Market Bridge in 1924 and shows the canal lock with the Cathedral tower and the spire of St. Alkmund's in the background. This interesting painting is not in the Goodey Collection but is owned privately.

Several of Harold's paintings were accepted at the Royal Academy and at least two of them were hung. These are "Gate Crag Grange" in Westmorland and "Skiddaw" in Cumberland. These paintings were selected from The Royal Institute of Painters in Watercolours. On Harold's "private view" ticket were printed the words "Touching Days" and on being asked what that meant, the artist explained that when most artists have finished their pictures they send them to be framed. From the framers, they go direct to the Academy, the result being that when the artist sees the finished article it sometimes looks not quite as he intended. On "Touching Days" he may go and touch up here and there to get the desired effect.

Harold's studio at his home in School Lane was situated in his lovely garden, which in spring and summer time was always a glorious sight, with an array of every kind of flower. The studio was glass-sided and roofed, almost like a greenhouse and here he would sit, peacefully painting his landscape watercolours. Chellaston village school was situated next door to his home and only a low brick wall separated the school playground from Harold's garden. Frequently footballs would arrive in the garden but were always returned by Mr Gresley with a cheerful word to the young players and no complaints. The head teacher, Mr Percy Willis-Francis, regularly invited Harold into the school to examine the children's artwork and to recommend any artistically gifted child who might achieve a scholarship to the Derby School of Art. Harold and Clara Gresley remained childless and this was a great pity because they were both very fond of children.

During World War II, it was necessary to form fire-watching parties to safeguard the village during the nightly air raids. Harold chaired most of the meetings, which took place in the school, and he took an active part in training the Stirrup Pump Teams. He also gave lectures on different known gases – their smell and remedies to be used if necessary.

An artist's studio may conjure up for some of us a depressing attic with sloping roof and an untidy appearance but Harold Gresley's town studio, right in the centre of Derby in St. James's Street was anything but depressing. The cheerful, cosy room had two large north windows, a warm fire, black curtains, a small dais, an easel and artist's materials. Here, Harold painted his portraits, or as he called them "speaking likenesses".

The following is an extract from the local paper describing two portraits, one of a little girl, Sue Dixon, and the other of the well-known Derby personality, Arthur Barlow:

Two Portraits

When I called in at Mr Gresley's studio the other day a most striking portrait of a little Derby girl caught my eye and held my attention for a long time. She is fair haired, blue eyed and serious with the solemnity that a five year old seems to combine with wonder.

Her chubby hands are folded placidly. Her dress is pale pink trimmed with tucks and lace, and the portrait is "a thing of beauty". Mr Gresley placed another portrait beside it – that of Mr Arthur Barlow. Knowing him, I can truthfully say the likeness is remarkable. He too is serious on the canvas – or perhaps "earnest" is a better word.

The two portraits – one with a splash of pink, the other dark with a tiny spot of colour here and there are delightful contrasts from the brush of a great artist.

Another of Harold's portraits was commissioned and painted for the Chamber of the Derbyshire County Council, where it now hangs, at Matlock. This portrait depicts Alderman Charles White. As well as his townscapes and portraits, Harold worked extensively in Derbyshire, especially in his beloved Trent Valley area. His watercolours of these pastoral scenes with the scurrying clouds and the ever-changing play of colours, reveal the strong influence of his father and grandfather. Harold's palette seems to have an extra vibrancy and is more lively, often with blue and green tones predominating, while father Frank's landscapes have a more yellowy, brown Autumnal effect. The appeal of Harold's work lies very much in its picturesque subjects and delicate colouring. He often used his father's sketchbook but painted in his own style, showing clarity of colours especially in water and skies.

In July 1945, at the annual sports day at Repton Preparatory School, Foremark Hall, Milton, two specially commissioned paintings by Harold Gresley were presented to the senior master Mr J F S Tullo, who was leaving after fourteen years, having been appointed to the Abbey Choir School at Westminster. The pictures depicted views of the interior and exterior of Foremark Church, for which Mr Tullo had done much to raise funds for restoration work.

At the fifty ninth Derby Sketching Club Exhibition in 1945, Harold was said to be the worthy successor to the late Ernest Townsend, who had been their leading portraitist until his death in 1944. Three of Harold's portraits executed in oils were displayed at the exhibition. One, entitled "Reverie", showed Mr A E Goodey looking deep in thought, while in complete contrast he also exhibited "Schooldays", showing Mary, a Friargate House schoolgirl, with her fresh youthful expression evocative of the springtime of life. The third portrait in the exhibition tells a very different story. This shows Henry Dumelow, an eighty six-year old Derby veteran of the Boer War. His lined and weather-beaten face seems to express memories of his earlier military days when he had taken part in the historic dash to relieve General Gordon at Khartoum. These portraits show clearly the remarkable skill of the artist to convey the various characteristics of his sitters.

At this time, Harold Gresley launched out boldly into portraiture, revealing a rare ability in capturing elusive expression and conveying it to canvas with masterly technique. Mr Goodey, the chairman of the Sketching Club, said that Mr Gresley would shine as a painter of child portraits. One of Harold's oil paintings entitled "The Convex Mirror", was purchased some years ago by the Friends of Derby Museum and Art Gallery. The 1945 painting is a self-portrait. He is shown in his studio and his face is set in an expression of deep concentration. It is possible he took his inspiration for this work from the famous "Giovanni Arnolfine & Giovanna Cenami" dated 1434 by Jan Van Eyck. During 1964, Harold served on the Derby Museum and Art Gallery sub-committee along with Mr Walker who had been a fellow student at the Derby School of Art. On very many occasions, Harold was called upon to judge painting at local exhibitions.

Harold Gresley (right) at Repton School in 1961 judging a painting competition.
Derby Evening Telegraph

Later in life, Harold had a studio at the rear of 22 Irongate (currently Sally Montague Hair Group), opposite Derby Cathedral. This was situated on the ground floor and is now part of the present shop.

Sadly, Harold was the last of the of the gifted artists in the Gresley family. He died on 10 July 1967 in the Royal Infirmary aged seventy-five. He had lived all his life at "Crow Tree House" in School Lane at Chellaston and his work had been exhibited at the Royal Academy, the Royal Institute and the Royal Watercolour Society exhibitions.

Although his gentle temperament might have robbed him of the power to portray the more spectacular awe-inspiring aspects of the Welsh mountains, he was successful in conveying that sense of timelessness in both mountains and sea.

Harold's artistic outlook was never in any sense of the term revolutionary, nevertheless he achieved through his talents a satisfaction for himself and much pleasure for others in following the more traditional paths of his art. He shared with his father a great love for the valley of the river Trent as it meanders through the villages of south Derbyshire. He was particularly sensitive to its quiet charm and I hope future generations will thank him for catching and preserving on paper the peacefulness of this area. For more than a century the Gresley family had been prominent figures in the artistic scene in Derbyshire and there can be few families that have produced such a succession of professional, talented painters. Their works survive to bear witness to a remarkable dynasty and surely the Gresleys are the best loved and most familiar family of artists in Derbyshire.

Harold painting Hollow Farm at Stanton by Bridge on 18th August 1955.
Derby Evening Telegraph

Selected Paintings by Harold Gresley

'The Convex Mirror' by Harold.
This 1945 oil painting is a self portrait.
Note his concentrated expression
and his palette & brushes.
This painting is possibly inspired
by 'The Arnolfini Marriage'
dated 1434 by Jan Van Eyck.

Derby Museums & Art Gallery

Hollow Farm, Wards Lane, Stanton by Bridge.

Watercolour portrait of
Clare Gresley painted by Harold.
Signed and dated 1920.

Watercolour portrait by Harold
of his wife Clare.
Signed and dated 1935.

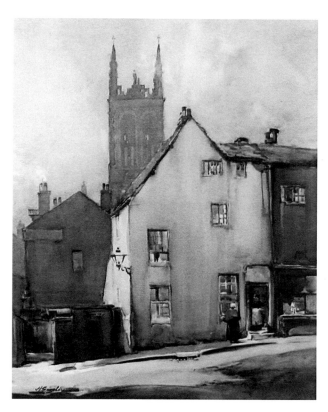

Old cottages at the corner of Darley Grove & Bridgegate 1938.
Derby Museums & Art Gallery

Queen Street, Derby 1926. Showing the Bull's Head & the Old Dolphin.
Note the power station in the background in the process of being built.
Derby Museums & Art Gallery

'The Village Street', Chellaston dated 1904. Painted by Harold
and presumably taken from his father Frank's sketch book.

Chellaston Village in 1912 showing the thatched Rose & Crown and the toll house in the distance.
Dated 1912 and probably taken from his father's sketch book.

Church Lane, Swarkestone.

South Derbyshire woodland scene.

Entitled 'Village Street', Chellaston 1900. Signed and dated 1951.

Swarkestone Bridge. Painted circa 1958.

Still life. Sweet Peas. Signed and dated 1910.

Still life. Roses in a bowl. Signed and dated 1912.

'Spitfire Patrol'. An unusual subject for Harold to paint.

River Dove, Mill Dale. Signed and dated 1928.

St. Wilfred's Church, Barrow on Trent.

St. James Church, Swarkestone.

Oil on canvas entitled 'Schooldays'.
Portrait of Mary,
Friar Gate House schoolgirl
This portrait was exhibited
at the 5th Derby Sketching Club
Exhibition in 1945.

Still life study of
summer flowers in
a pottery vase.

Bluebell Wood, Calke Park. Note the rabbits near the tree roots.

Jasmine Cottage, Derby Road, Chellaston c.1955.
This house was occupied for a time by Cuthbert's son Kenneth Gresley.

Pingle Lane, Swarkestone.

Marston Mongomery Church. Signed and dated 1882 by Alice Gresley.
Alice was the daughter of James Stevens Gresley.

Extracts from the Gresley Family Tree

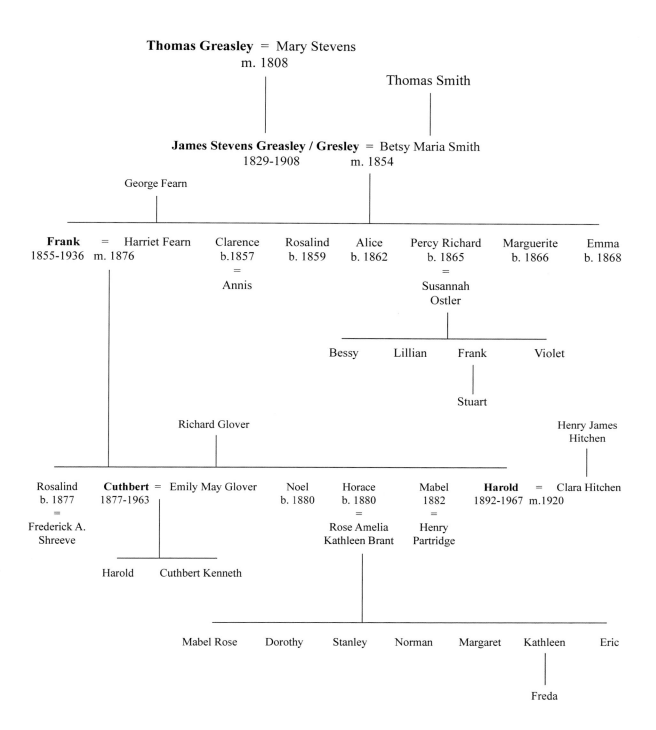

Audrey Longdon was born in 1924, the daughter of the late Mr and Mrs Allan Walton. She was also the granddaughter of William Croall Walton who was the much respected headmaster of Allenton School for 23 years. He was greatly admired by Audrey and, I believe, was the inspiration for the book she wrote later in life, "Early Allenton and its Environs", also published by Chellaston History Group.

Audrey herself was very intelligent and had many absorbing interests. For many years she was a member of the Chellaston History Group. Her passion was reading the biographies and autobiographies of interesting historical characters. On many occasions whilst travelling on the bus to Derby we had interesting conversations on various historical subjects, so much so, that we were often surprised to find the bus had arrived at our destination in what appeared to be a very short time.

Audrey was very diminutive and had an extremely good memory for detail. Often when discussing an historical T.V. programme Audrey would say, "They've got it wrong, or such and such a person never did that" or "she did not marry him".

Audrey left school when only fourteen years old and worked in the Payroll Department at Rolls Royce for a number of years. During the war the Payroll was transferred to Belper and she found herself travelling there and back through the blackout. During her employment at Rolls Royce she became acquainted with a number of senior people in the company and having an inquisitive nature, learned their background and history.

After the war she left Rolls Royce to undertake teacher training and entered the profession. She taught for many years at Chellaston Infants School in School Lane and transferred later to the new Junior School. Another interest was Scottish Dancing, which she taught for a number of years, forming a successful dance class at the Junior School.

Another of her interests was in the life and works of the leading local artistic Gresley family. Over many years she gathered a great deal of information and a large number of photographs. From this she gave talks on the subject, and was finally persuaded to write and publish a book on the history of this talented family. She completed her research and wrote the script for this book, but sadly, died before it could be published. In her memory, her daughter Cathryn took on the task and has now completed the work.

Arthur Shardlow
Chairman
Chellaston History Group

Chellaston.

Nr Derby.

March 22nd 1916

My dear Percy.

Rose has sent me your letter
I really hope that nothing will
happen to the Southern Cross as you
would feel a bit lonesome without
it.

I feel ashamed that I have neglected
writing to you so long. People tell
me I am a bad correspondent.

I often think of you down under &
wonder what it is like. I don't
suppose I shall ever see for myself.
As you know I am quite alone
now it seems very strange &
a weary while waiting here &
wondering day by day what is happening.
I really don't know what I should
do if anything happened to Harold.
I have spent the latter part of my
life for him & hoping as I may say
to live part of it over again, when
he got fairly going in his career.
He was still at the School when the War broke out.

He is very clever & can draw or paint
anything. Portraits, landscape & anything
he sees. I am very glad he managed
to paint a wonderfully good portrait of
his mother before she died. He was
only 19 when he did it.

He has been to the Dardanelles & got
damaged there but soon got well again
& is now in France. in the 1st Battalion
Royal Fusiliers. He got his stripes a
few days ago & is now Lance Corporal.
He could have had promotion over
12 months ago but would not take it
until he was on active service.

I am glad to hear your boy Frank is
coming out & hope I shall see him &
that he will come safely through.

I do not think somehow that the War
will last so very much longer as I
think the Germans have about shot their
bolt & it looks as if they would soon
have trouble with their own people at
home when they find out how
they have been gulled & deceived.
& both Bulgaria & Turkey would be
glad to get out of it if they could.
Give my love to your wife & children
I should like to see them all but
I am afraid that will never be. You
see I am getting old now. I shall be